My First Book about the Alphabet of Coastal Animals

Amazing Animal Books
Children's Picture Books
By Molly Davidson
Mendon Cottage Books

JD-Biz Publishing

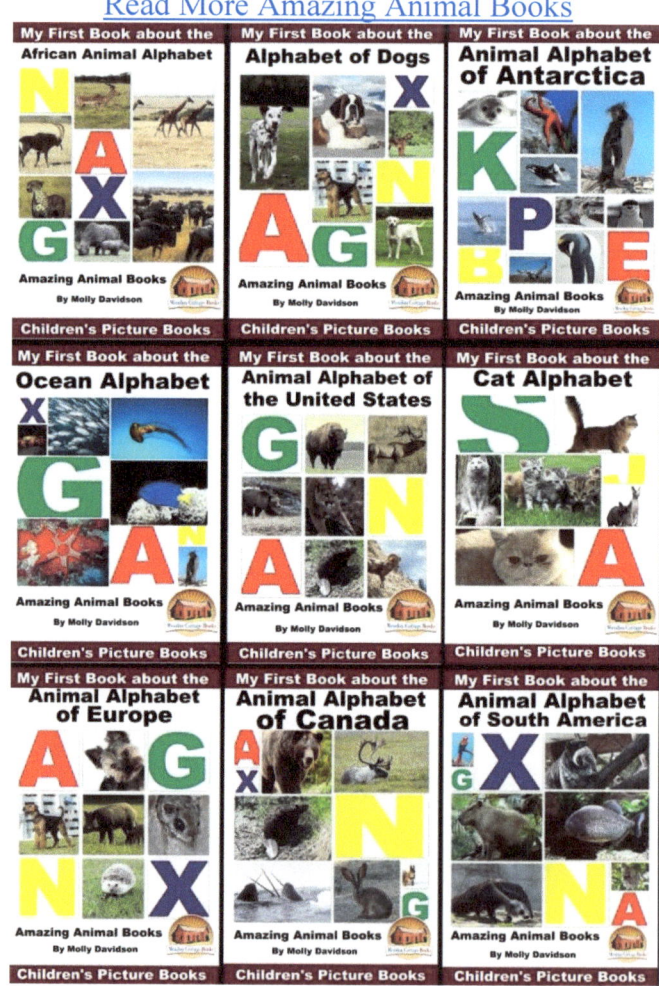

Purchase at Amazon.com

Download Free Books!
http://MendonCottageBooks.com

Introduction

The coast is a very popular place for all types of animals.

Birds love the coast because there is always food.

Many ocean animals will come to dry land to lay their eggs.

 **is for an Anemone.**

Sea anemones can be found living all over in the World's oceans; the biggest live in the tropical coastal waters.

They catch fish as they swim by and sting them with their tentacles.

A is also for an Archerfish.

They are found on the coasts of India, Australia, and the Philippines.

Archerfish kill their prey by shooting water above the surface of the water at it; they usually hit on the first try.

 is for a Bottlenose Dolphin.

Bottlenose dolphins prefer to stay in the shallow, warmer, coastal waters.

They travel in large groups, sometimes between 100 - 2,000 dolphins.

They can swim up to 25 mph and live between 20 - 45 years.

B is also for Brachyura, the scientific name for a Crab.

Crab like to live in rocky pools or the coral reefs of shallow coastal waters.

They have a hard shell which helps protect them from predators, as well as two front claws that they use to catch prey.

C is for a Clownfish.

Clownfish can be found living in the coral reefs of tropical coastal waters.

They lay hundreds, sometimes thousands, of eggs close to their sea anemone homes. The eggs take about one week to hatch.

C is also for Coral.

Coral is a living animal, which looks like a spongy rock on the bottom of costal shores.

They are extremely important to ocean animals, because many build their homes in them, use them as a hiding spot, and many fish also gather in the reefs.

D is for a Dugong.

Dugongs live in the shallow waters around Australia and Indonesia.

They are also called sea cows, and eat ocean grasses, plants, and flowers.

They usually live for 50 - 70 years.

 **is for an Eel.**

There are over 400 different species of eel, which can be found in all the World's oceans.

Eels look like a snake, but they are a fish.

They can swim forward and backwards, and travel on land for a short distance.

F

is for a Flamingo.

Flamingos live in flocks of up to 200 birds, in the shallow waters of South America, Africa, and warm areas of Europe and Asia.

The color of a flamingo's feathers is based on what they eat, most pink flamingos eat shrimp.

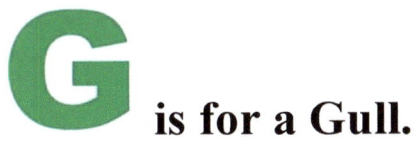

G is for a Gull.

Gulls are seen fly over most ocean coastlines looking for food to eat.

They will drop mollusks on the rocks to break open their shells, so they can eat them.

H

 **is for a Hermit Crab.**

Hermit crabs live mostly in the shallow waters of all the oceans of the World.

They have a soft underbody that they cover with a shell, as they grow they have to find new shells to live in.

There are over 500 species of hermit crab.

H is also for Holothuroidea, the scientific name for a Sea Cucumber.

Sea cucumbers like to live in the shallow ocean waters, sometimes digging into the ocean's sandy bottom.

They eat algae and fish waste, which they pick up with a few tentacles by their mouths.

I is for an Indian Sea Star.

Indian sea stars can be found in the coral reefs of the Indian and Pacific Oceans.

They have two stomachs which help them digest clams and oysters.

If they get hurt they can grow new arms.

J is for a Japanese Glass Shrimp.

Japanese Glass Shrimp are found off the coast of the Toyoma Bay in Japan.

They are a little pink, then they turn clear, like glass, when they are cooked.

 is for a Kune's Chromodoris.

Kune's chromodoris lives in the coral reefs of the Indian and Western Pacific Oceans.

These brightly colored sea slugs ooze acid from their tentacles that stings predators.

They swim very slowly through the water.

L is for a Leopard Seal.

Leopard seals live on the icy coasts of Antarctica, and eat penguins.

They have a thick lay of fat, called blubber, which helps keep them warm as they swim in the frigid ocean water.

L is also for a Loggerhead Sea Turtle.

Loggerhead turtles live in the tropical coastal waters.

They will lay their eggs on the sandy beaches of the coasts.

 **is for a Manta Ray.**

Manta rays, a relative of the shark, like the warmer, coastal waters around coral reefs.

They can grow to be up to 25 feet (9 m) wide!

M is also for Mudskippers.

Mudskippers live in seaweed and tide pools where the ocean tide flows in and out.

They use their pectoral fins to walk on land.

They can breathe though their skin when it's wet.

 **is for a Necklace Giant Clam.**

Necklace giant clams stay in one place their whole lives, they can be found in the coral reefs of the Indian and Pacific Oceans.

They survive on the algae that float through the reefs, and some live to be 100 years old.

O

is for Otariinae, the scientific name for a Sea Lion.

Sea lions like to live on rocky coastlines.

They have flippers instead of feet which helps them glide quicker through the water.

Their teeth are used for tearing more than chewing.

P is for Puffins.

Puffins live on the rocky shores of the Northern Arctic.

They are excellent fliers, and have been known to fly up to 55 mph.

They dive into the water to get food; they can be underwater for up to 2 minutes.

P is also for a Pelican.

Pelicans like to live on the coast where there is plenty of fish to catch.

They can have a wingspan of up to 10 feet.

 **is for a Queen Triggerfish.**

![Queen Triggerfish]

James St. John © <u>Wikimedia Commons</u>

Queen triggerfish live in the coral reefs of the Atlantic Ocean.

They will raise their top fin as a warning for others to stay away.

 **R** is for a Rockhopper Penguin.

Rockhopper penguins live on the rocky coasts of Antarctica, where they jump across the rocks instead of sliding on their bellies

S is for a Sea Dragon.

Sea dragons can be found in the coastal waters around Australia.

They are good at camouflaging in the sea weed, where they wait for prey, like shrimp, plankton, crustaceans, and small fish.

T is for a Tricolored Heron.

The tricolored heron lives along the coast of the southern United States down into Mexico, Peru, and Brazil.

It runs in the shallow coastal waters, grabbing its food of crustaceans, reptiles, fish, and insects, as it goes.

U is for an Urchin.

Sea urchins are related to sand dollars, and live in coral reefs all over the World.

They use their spikes for digging in the sand for protection and to capture food.

 **is for a Vagabond Butterflyfish.**

Dr. Dwayne Meadows © <u>Wikimedia Commons</u>

Vagabond Butterflyfish live in the coral reefs around Asia, Eastern Africa, and Australia.

They eat algae, coral, worms, and crustaceans.

 **is for a Walrus.**

Walruses are found living on the shores around the icy, Arctic Circle.

They are very social; this is why they live in groups of up to 1,000.

They dive down to the dark ocean floor where they eat.

Y

is for a Yellowfin Goatfish.

Yellowfin Goatfish live in the shallow waters of the Caribbean and Western Atlantic Ocean.

They use their chins to dig into the sand to find worms, crustaceans, small fish, and sea stars.

 **is for a Zebra Lionfish.**

Zebra lionfish live in the coral reefs of the Indian and Eastern Pacific Oceans.

Their feathery fins are highly venomous.

During the day they hide in caves, usually upside down.

Conclusion

I hope you have enjoyed reading about all the amazing animals that live on the coast.

One more fact: There is over 221,000 miles of coastline in the World, plenty of space for all who live there.

Our books are available at

1. Amazon.com

2. Barnes and Noble

3. Itunes

4. Kobo

5. Smashwords

6. Google Play Books

Download Free Books!
http://MendonCottageBooks.com

Publisher

JD-Biz Corp

P O Box 374

Mendon, Utah 84325

http://www.jd-biz.com/

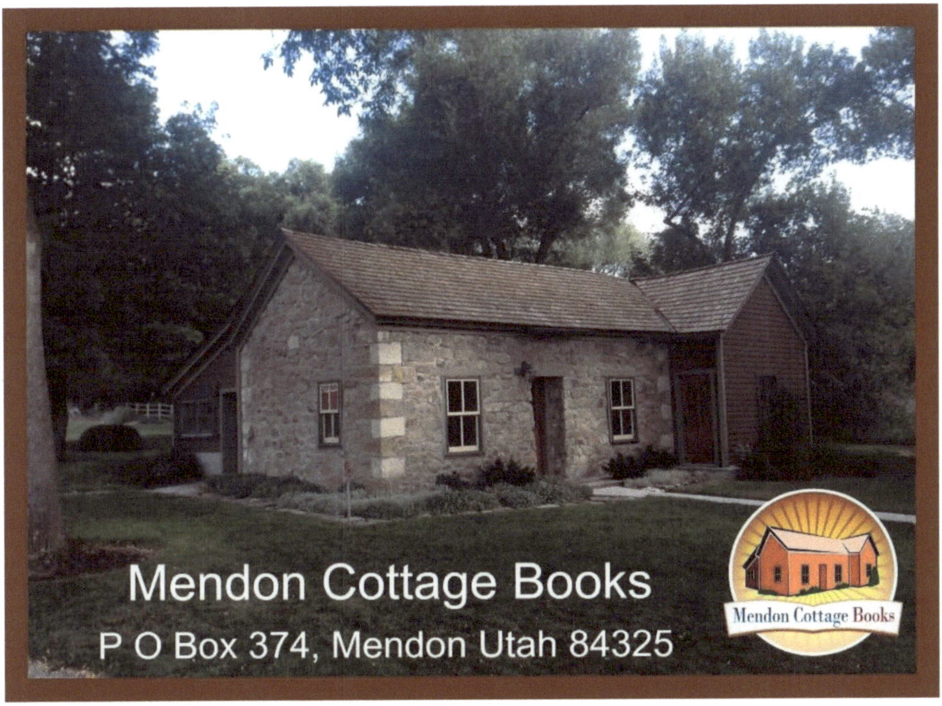

Mendon Cottage Books

P O Box 374, Mendon Utah 84325